Handkerchief Edgings
& Keepsakes™

General Information

Many of the products used in this pattern book can be purchased from local craft, fabric and variety stores, or from the Annie's Attic Needlecraft Catalog (see Customer Service information on page 23).

Contents

2 Church Doll

4 Rose Bud Wall Pocket

5 Baby Bonnet/Bride's Hankie

6 Stairway to Heaven Angel

8 Flower Garland Sachet

9 Hunny Bunny Sachet

11 Hankie Dress

14 Sweet Dreams Pillow

17 Springtime Bouquet Vase

18 Flirty Fans Flower

19 Tiny Tiaras Flower

20 Romantic Ruffles Flower

21 Beaded Art Nouveau Bag

24 Stitch Guide

Church Doll

SKILL LEVEL

EASY

FINISHED SIZES
Edging: ½ inch wide
Doll: Approximately 8½ to 11 inches tall, depending on size of handkerchief

MATERIALS
- Size 10 crochet cotton:
   100 yds desired edging color
- Size 10/1.15mm steel crochet hook
- Lady's or man's handkerchief
- Polyester fiberfill

SPECIAL STITCH
Cluster (cl): Yo, insert hook in ch, yo, pull lp through, yo, pull through 2 lps on hook, yo, insert hook in same ch, yo, pull lp through, yo, pull through 2 lps on hook, yo, pull through all 3 lps on hook.

INSTRUCTIONS
EDGING
Rnd 1: Place slip knot on hook and insert hook through fabric on outer edge of handkerchief, yo, pull lp through, yo, complete as sc, ch 3, **cl** (*see Special Stitch*) in 3rd ch from hook, sp sts about ½ inch apart, [sc, ch 3, cl in 3rd ch from hook] around, join with sl st in beg sc. Fasten off.

BONNET
Row 1: Ch 12, join with sl st in beg ch to form ring, **ch 4** (*counts as first dc and ch-1 sp*), dc in ring, [ch 1, dc in ring] 10 times, turn. (*12 dc, 11 ch sps*)

Rows 2–6: Ch 5 (*counts as first dc and ch-2 sp*), dc in next st, [ch 2, dc in next st] across, turn.

Row 7: Ch 1, sc in first st, [ch 3, cl in 3rd ch from hook, sc in next st] across, for **tie**, ch 30. Fasten off.

For **2nd tie**, join with sl st in first st of row 7, ch 30. Fasten off.

FINISHING
1. Fold top ¼ of handkerchief to front.

2. Place small amount fiberfill in center of fold. Gather fabric around fiberfill to form head, tie 24-inch strand crochet cotton tightly around bottom of head, wrap several times and secure.

3. Pull fabric out on each side of head to form arms. Tie 12-inch strand crochet cotton around arm about ⅓ length of arm from end. Fold end back up over where tied and tie ½ inch from fold to form hand. Rep on other side for other hand.

4. Tie 24-inch strand crochet cotton around waist below arms.

5. Place Bonnet on head and tie to secure. ∎

Rose Bud
Wall Pocket

SKILL LEVEL

INTERMEDIATE

FINISHED SIZES
Edging: ½ inch wide
Wall Pocket: 6½ x 7½ inches

MATERIALS
- Size 10 crochet cotton:
   75 yds each green and pink
- Size 10/1.15mm steel crochet hook
- Sewing needle
- Lady's white handkerchief
- Matching sewing thread
- Spray starch

SPECIAL STITCHES
Cluster (cl): Yo, insert hook in designated ch, yo, pull lp through, yo, pull through 2 lps on hook, yo, insert hook in same ch, yo, pull lp through, yo, pull through 2 lps on hook, yo, pull through all 3 lps on hook.

Picot: Ch 3, sc in top of last cl made.

INSTRUCTIONS
EDGING
Row 1: With green, [ch 4, dc in 4th ch from hook] number of times needed to fit around outer edge of handkerchief, ending in odd number of ch sps. Fasten off.

Row 2: Join pink with sc in first ch sp, *(dc, {ch 2, sl st, ch 2, dc} twice) in next ch sp, sc in next ch sp, rep from * across. Fasten off.

ROSE
For **petals**, with pink, [ch 3, (dc, ch 3, sl st) in 3rd ch from hook] 3 times, [ch 3, (2 dc, ch 3, sl st) in 3rd ch from hook] 5 times, [ch 3, (3 dc, ch 3, sl st) in 3rd ch from hook] 6 times. Fasten off. *(14 petals)*

Roll petals to form Rose; tack in place at base of sts.

LEAF SPRAY
MAKE 2.
With green, ch 9, for **first Leaf**, (**cl**—see Special Stitches, **picot**—see Special Stitches, ch 4, sl st) in 4th ch from hook, for **2nd Leaf**, ch 7, (cl, picot, ch 4, sl st) in 4th ch from hook, sl st in each of next 3 chs of ch-7, for **3rd Leaf**, ch 5, (dc, picot, ch 4, sl st) in 4th ch from hook, sl st in next ch of ch-5, sl st in same ch as first cl was made, sl st in each rem ch of ch-9. Fasten off.

POCKET
1. Sew Edging to outer edge of handkerchief.

2. Matching 1 corner to opposite corner, fold handkerchief in half, forming a triangle with fold at bottom; press.

3. Fold left-hand lower corner over to right-hand straight edge of triangle; press.

4. Fold right-hand lower corner over to left-hand straight edge of triangle; press.

5. Fold top front corner down over folded side corners, press; tack in place.

6. Sew Rose and Leaf Sprays to center of last folded corner as shown in photo. ∎

Baby Bonnet/Bride's Hankie

SKILL LEVEL
■■□□ INTERMEDIATE

FINISHED SIZE
Edging is ¾ inch wide

MATERIALS
- Size 10 crochet cotton: 200 yds blue or pink
- Size 10/1.15mm steel crochet hook
- Sewing needle
- ⅝-inch-wide blue or pink ribbon: 40 inches
- Lady's white handkerchief with prepunched holes around outer edge
- ½-inch buttons: 2
- White sewing thread

PATTERN NOTES
Join with slip stitch as indicated unless otherwise stated.

If you cannot find a handkerchief with prepunched holes, place slip knot on hook and insert hook through fabric on outer edge of handkerchief, yarn over, pull loop through, yarn over, complete as single crochet, work in same manner evenly spaced around outer edge as indicted in pattern.

SPECIAL STITCHES
Love knot: Pull up a ½-inch lp on hook, yo, pull lp through, sc in back strand of long lp *(see Fig. 1)*.

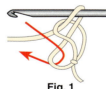
Fig. 1 Love Knot

Double love knot: *Pull up a ½-inch lp on hook, yo, pull lp through, sc in back strand of long lp *(see Fig. 1)*, rep from * *(see Fig. 2)*.

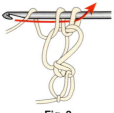
Fig. 2 Double Love Knot

INSTRUCTIONS
EDGING
Rnd 1: Working through holes around outer edge of **Hankie** *(see Pattern Notes)*, join with sc in any hole, **double love knot** *(see Special Stitches)*, evenly sp sts ¼ inch apart, (sc, double love knot) around with (sc, double love knot) twice in each corner hole, **join** *(see Pattern Notes)* in beg sc.

Rnd 2: Love knot *(see Special Stitches)*, [sc in center of next double love knot, love knot] around, join in beg sc. Fasten off.

BONNET
1. Fold Hankie in half. Baste across Hankie 1 inch from fold to form casing. Pull 12-inch piece of ribbon through casing, pull to gather; tie ribbon ends into a bow.

2. For **tie**, fold down end of 14-inch piece of ribbon 1½ inches. Tack folded end to bottom front corner of Bonnet at an angle *(see photo)*. Sew 1 button to folded end; trim other end. Rep on other side of Bonnet with rem 14-inch piece of ribbon. ■

Stairway to Heaven Angel

SKILL LEVEL

EASY

FINISHED SIZE
Edging: ½ inch wide
Doll: Approximately 7 to 8½ inches tall, depending on size of handkerchief

MATERIALS
- Size 10 crochet cotton:
    100 yds desired edging color
    25 yds yellow
    24 inches white
- Size 10/1.15mm steel crochet hook
- Sewing needle
- ½-inch-wide matching ribbon: 24 inches
- Lady's or Christmas-theme handkerchief
- Sewing thread to match edging color
- Polyester fiberfill
- Fabric glue

SPECIAL STITCHES
Picot: Ch 3, sl st in 3rd ch from hook.

Cluster (cl): Yo, insert hook in ch, yo, pull lp through, yo, pull through 2 lps on hook, yo, insert hook in same ch, yo, pull lp through, yo, pull through 2 lps on hook, yo, pull through all 3 lps on hook.

INSTRUCTIONS
EDGING
Row 1: Ch 2, 3 sc in 2nd ch from hook, turn. *(3 sc)*

Row 2: Ch 1, 3 sc in first st, leaving rem sts unworked, turn.

Rep row 2 until Edging fits around entire handkerchief when placed ½ inch from outer edge.

STAR FLOWER
With yellow, ch 3, (dc, **picot**—see Special Stitches, ch 3, sl st) in 3rd ch from hook, (ch 3, dc, picot, ch 3, sl st) 4 times in same ch as first dc. Fasten off.

HALO
Rnd 1: With edging color, ch 6, sl st in beg ch to form ring, **ch 4** *(counts as first dc and ch-1 sp)*, (dc, ch 1) 11 times in ring, join with sl st in 3rd ch of beg ch-4. *(12 dc, 12 ch sps)*

Rnd 2: Ch 5 *(counts as first dc and ch-2 sp)*, (dc, ch 2) in each st around, join in 3rd ch of beg ch 5. Fasten off for lady's handkerchief. **Do not fasten off** for Christmas-theme handkerchief.

Rnd 3: For **lady's handkerchief**, join yellow with sc in first st, ch 3, **cl** *(see Special Stitches)* in 3rd ch from hook, [sc in next st, ch 3, cl in 3rd ch from hook] around, join with sl st in beg sc. Fasten off.

Rnd 3: For **Christmas-theme handkerchief**, ch 1, sc in first st, ch 3, **cl** *(see Special Stitches)* in 3rd ch from hook, [sc in next st, ch 3, cl in 3rd ch from hook] around, join with sl st in beg sc. Fasten off.

FINISHING

1. Sew Edging around handkerchief ½ inch from outer edge.

2. Matching 1 corner to opposite corner, fold handkerchief in half, forming a triangle with fold at top.

3. Place small amount fiberfill in center of fold. Gather fabric around fiberfill to form head, tie white crochet cotton tightly around bottom of head, wrap several times and secure.

4. Pull top corners of handkerchief up to form wings.

5. Tie an 18-inch piece of ribbon around waist below wings and tie ends into a bow at back.

6. Pull 1 end of rem ribbon through wings below neck and above waist tie, pull until ends are even on each side. Tie ends into a knot 1 inch from ends and glue star to center of knot. Trim ends into a "V."

7. Glue Halo to back of head. ∎

Flower Garland Sachet

SKILL LEVEL

INTERMEDIATE

FINISHED SIZES
Edging: ¾ inch wide
Sachet: 4 inches across

MATERIALS
- Size 10 crochet cotton: 200 yds coordinating color
- Size 10/1.15mm steel crochet hook
- Sewing needle
- ½-inch-wide coordinating ribbon: 24 inches
- Lady's floral handkerchief
- Scented oil or perfume
- Matching sewing thread
- Spray starch
- Polyester fiberfill

INSTRUCTIONS
EDGING
Rnd 1: Place slip knot on hook and insert hook through fabric on outer edge of handkerchief, yo, pull lp through, yo, complete as sc, ch 7, (sl st, ch 3, dc, ch 2, sl st) 5 times in 3rd ch from hook, ch 4, [sc in handkerchief ½ inch from last sc, ch 7, (sl st, ch 3, dc, ch 2, sl st) in 3rd ch from hook, ch 4] around outer edge of handkerchief, join with sl st in beg sc. Fasten off.

SACHET
1. Fold each corner of handkerchief to center. Sew ½ inch from edge of each fold to form a casing.

2. Pull 1 end of ribbon through each casing. Scent fiberfill with oil or perfume; place desired amount into center of handkerchief and pull ribbon ends to gather sachet around fiberfill.

3. Pull each corner of handkerchief down over casing. Tie ends of ribbon into a bow. Tie knot in end of each ribbon end. ■

Hunny Bunny Sachet

SKILL LEVEL

INTERMEDIATE

FINISHED SIZES
Edging: ¼ inch wide
Bunny: 4½ to 5½ inches long depending on size of handkerchief

MATERIALS
- Size 10 crochet cotton:
    150 yds desired color
    5 yds each black and desired rosebud color
- Size 10/1.15mm steel crochet hook
- Sewing needle
- Lady's floral handkerchief
- Spray starch
- Polyester fiberfill
- Matching thread
- Craft glue or hot-glue gun

PATTERN NOTE
Join with a slip stitch as indicated unless otherwise stated.

SPECIAL STITCH
Cluster (cl): Yo, insert hook in ch, yo, pull lp through, yo, pull through 2 lps on hook, yo, insert hook in same ch, yo, pull lp through, yo, pull through 2 lps on hook, yo, pull through all 3 lps on hook.

INSTRUCTIONS
EDGING
Rnd 1: With Edging color, place slip knot on hook and insert hook through fabric on outer edge of handkerchief, yo, pull lp through, yo, complete as sc, ch 3, sp sts about ¼ inch apart, (sc, ch 3) around outer edge of handkerchief with (sc, ch 3) twice in each corner, **join** *(see Pattern Note)* in beg sc.

Rnd 2: Ch 1, (sc, ch 2, hdc) in each ch sp around with (sc, {ch 2, hdc, sc} twice, ch 2, hdc) in each corner ch sp, join in beg sc. Fasten off.

EYE
MAKE 2.
With black, ch 3, **cl** *(see Special Stitch)* in 3rd ch from hook, ch 1. Fasten off.

NOSE & WHISKERS
Cut 3 strands black, each 6 inches long. Holding all strands tog, tie knot in center. Trim ends even.

ROSEBUD
With rosebud color, [ch 3, (hdc, ch 3, sl st) in 3rd ch from hook] 8 times. Fasten off.

Roll into rose shape, tack tog at bottom.

FINISHING
1. Spray handkerchief with starch, press.

2. For Bunny, match 1 corner to opposite corner and fold handkerchief in half, forming a triangle. Roll small amount of fiberfill into a tube and place inside fold with ends of fiberfill tube 2 inches from each end of handkerchief.

3. Starting at fold, roll handkerchief up; fold in half. Fold points back about 4 inches. Tie strand of Edging color around all thicknesses of folded points and tube to form head *(see photo)*. Unstuffed points will form ears at top of head.

4. Tack or glue Rosebud at base of ears.

5. Tack or glue Eyes, Nose and Whiskers to face as shown in photo. ∎

Hankie Dress

SKILL LEVEL

INTERMEDIATE

FINISHED SIZES
Edging: 1 inch wide
Dress: 10½ inches tall

MATERIALS
- Size 10 crochet cotton:
    200 yds blue
- Size 7/1.65mm steel crochet hook
- Sewing needle
- ⅜-inch-wide white ribbon: 18 inches
- Lady's white handkerchief with prepunched holes around outer edge
- Florist's wire
- White sewing thread
- Spray starch

PATTERN NOTES
Join with a slip stitch as indicated unless otherwise stated.

Chain-3 at beginning of round counts as first double crochet unless otherwise stated.

If you cannot find a handkerchief with pre-punched holes, place slip knot on hook and insert hook through fabric on outer edge of handkerchief, yarn over, pull loop through, yarn over, complete as single crochet, work in same manner evenly spaced around outer edge as indicted in pattern.

SPECIAL STITCHES
Cluster (cl): Yo, insert hook in designated ch, yo, pull lp through, yo, pull through 2 lps on hook, yo, insert hook in same ch, yo, pull lp through, yo, pull through 2 lps on hook, yo, pull through all 3 lps on hook.

Picot: Ch 3, sc in top of last cl made.

INSTRUCTIONS
EDGING
Rnd 1: Working through holes around outer edge of **handkerchief** (see Pattern Notes), join with sc in any corner hole, (ch 3, sc) 3 times in same hole, ch 3, sk next 2 holes, [sc in next hole, ch 3, sk next 2 holes] around with (sc, {ch 3, sc} 3 times) in each corner hole, **join** (see Pattern Notes) in beg sc.

Rnds 2–4: Sl st in next ch sp, ch 1, sc in same sp, ch 4, (sc, ch 4) in each ch sp around, join in beg sc.

Rnd 5: Sl st in next ch sp, ch 1, (sc, ch 3, sc) in same sp and in each ch sp around, join in beg sc. Fasten off.

ROSE
For **petals**, [ch 3, (dc, ch 3, sl st) in 3rd ch from hook] 3 times, [ch 3, (2 dc, ch 3, sl st) in 3rd ch from hook] 5 times, [ch 3, (3 dc, ch 3, sl st) in 3rd ch from hook] 6 times. Fasten off. *(14 petals)*

Roll petals to form Rose; tack in place at base of sts.

LEAF SPRAY
MAKE 2.
Ch 9, for **first Leaf**, (**cl**—*see Special Stitches*, **picot**—*see Special Stitches*, ch 4, sl st) in 4th ch from hook, for **2nd Leaf**, ch 7 (cl, picot, ch 4, sl st) in 4th ch from hook, sl st in each of next 3 chs of ch-9, for **3rd Leaf**, ch 5, (dc, picot, ch 4, sl st) in 4th ch from hook, sl st in each of last 2 chs of ch-9. Fasten off.

BODICE
Rnd 1: Ch 50, join in beg ch to form ring, **ch 3** (*see Pattern Notes*), dc in **back bar** (*see Fig. 1*) of each ch around, join in 3rd ch of beg ch-3. *(50 dc)*

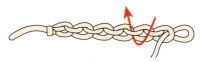

Fig. 1
Back Bar of Chain

Rnd 2: Ch 3, dc in each of next 6 sts, for **armhole**, sk next 12 sts, dc in each of next 13 sts, for **armhole**, sk next 12 sts, dc in each of last 6 sts, join in 3rd ch of beg ch-3. *(26 dc)*

Rnd 3: Ch 3, dc in each st around, join in 3rd ch of beg ch-3.

Rnd 4: Ch 3, dc in each of next 4 sts, **dc dec** (*see Stitch Guide*) in next 2 sts, dc in each of next 12 sts, dc dec in next 2 sts, dc in each of last 5 sts, join in 3rd ch of beg ch-3. *(24 dc)*

Rnd 5: Ch 3, dc in next st, dc dec in next 2 sts, [dc in each of next 2 sts, dc dec in next 2 sts] around, join in 3rd ch of beg ch-3. *(18 dc)*

Rnd 6: Ch 3, dc in each st around, join in 3rd ch of beg ch-3.

Rnd 7: Ch 3, 2 dc in next st, [dc in next st, 2 dc in next st] around, join in 3rd ch of beg ch-3. *(27 dc)*

Rnd 8: Ch 3, 2 dc in next st, [dc in next st, 2 dc in next st] 5 times, tr in next st, 3 tr in next st, tr in next st, [2 dc in next st, dc in next st] 6 times, join in 3rd ch of beg ch-3. Fasten off.

RUFFLE
Rnd 1: Working on opposite side of starting ch in **back lps** (*see Stitch Guide*) of chs, join with sc in first st, ch 3, sk next ch, [sc in next ch, ch 3, sk next ch] around, join in beg sc. *(25 ch sps)*

Rnds 2 & 3: Sl st in each of next 2 chs of next ch-3, ch 1, sc in same sp, ch 3, [sc in next ch sp, ch 3] around, join in beg sc. Fasten off at end of last rnd.

FINISHING
1. Matching 1 corner to opposite corner, fold handkerchief in half, forming a triangle, press. Fold each side point back to meet bottom point, press. Pleat each side and press.

2. Sew Rose to center front of handkerchief (*see photo*). Sew 1 Leaf Spray to each side of Rose.

3. Spray Bodice with starch; shape and let dry.

4. Insert top of handkerchief into bottom of Bodice, sew to secure (*see photo*).

5. Tie ribbon around waist of Bodice with bow in back.

6. Shape florist's wire into a hanger shape. Place dress on hanger. ■

Sweet Dreams PILLOW

SKILL LEVEL

EASY

FINISHED SIZES
Edging: ¾ inch wide
Pillow: 10½ inches across, not including edging

MATERIALS
- Size 10 crochet cotton:
    150 yds each blue and yellow
- Size 7/1.65mm steel crochet hook
- Sewing needle
- 10½-inch-square lady's handkerchiefs: 2
- ½-inch decorative shank button
- White sewing thread
- Spray starch
- Polyester fiberfill

PATTERN NOTES
Join with a slip stitch as indicated unless otherwise stated.

Chain-3 at beginning of rounds counts as first double crochet unless otherwise stated.

INSTRUCTIONS
EDGING
MAKE 2.
Row 1: With blue, [ch 4, dc in 4th ch from hook] number of times needed to fit around outer edge of handkerchief, ending in odd number of ch sps. Fasten off.

Row 2: Join yellow with sc in first ch sp, [ch 2, (3 dc, ch 2, 3 dc) in next ch sp, ch 2, sc in next ch sp] across. Fasten off.

Row 3: Join blue with sc in first ch sp, *ch 3, sk next dc, sc in next dc, ch 3, (sc, ch 3, sc) in next ch sp, ch 3, sk next dc, sc in next dc, ch 3, sk next dc, sc in next ch sp**, sc in next ch sp, rep from * across, ending last rep at **. Fasten off.

Sew 1 Edging around outside edge of each handkerchief.

LACE MEDALLION
Rnd 1: With blue, ch 6, **join** (see Pattern Notes) in beg ch to form ring, **ch 3** (see Pattern Notes), 17 dc in ring, join in 3rd ch of beg ch 3. *(18 dc)*

Rnd 2: Ch 5 *(counts as first dc and ch-2 sp)*, dc in same st, ch 1, sk next st, *(dc, ch 2, dc) in next st, ch 1, sk next st, rep from * around, join in 3rd ch of beg ch-5. Fasten off. *(18 dc, 9 ch-2 sps, 9 ch-1 sps)*

Rnd 3: Join yellow with sc in any ch-1 sp, ch 2, (3 dc, ch 2, 3 dc) in next ch-2 sp, ch 2, [sc in next ch-1 sp, ch 2, (3 dc, ch 2, 3 dc) in next ch-2 sp, ch 2] around, join in beg sc. *(54 dc, 27 ch-2 sps, 9 sc)*

Rnd 4: Join blue with sc in first ch-2 sp, *ch 3, sk next dc, sc in next dc, ch 3, (sc, ch 3, sc) in next ch sp, ch 3, sk next dc, sc in next dc, ch 3, sk next dc, sc in next ch sp**, sc in next ch sp, rep from * across, ending last rep at **, join in beg sc. Fasten off.

FINISHING
1. With RS facing, place 1 handkerchief on top of the other with corners on top handkerchief centered between corners of bottom one.

2. Sew handkerchiefs tog across straight edges leaving corners unsewn, stuffing with fiberfill before closing.

3. Place Medallion at center of top handkerchief and sew button to center of Medallion through all thicknesses of pillow. ■

Springtime Bouquet Vase

SKILL LEVEL

INTERMEDIATE

FINISHED SIZE
Edging is 1 inch wide

MATERIALS
- Size 10 crochet cotton: 200 yds green
- Size 10/1.15mm steel crochet hook
- Sewing needle
- Green 1½-inch-wide ribbon: 1 yd
- 4-inch-tall x 16½-inch-circumference ivy bowl with neck
- Lady's green floral handkerchief
- Green sewing thread
- Spray starch

SPECIAL STITCHES
Cluster (cl): Yo, insert hook in designated ch, yo, pull lp through, yo, pull through 2 lps on hook, yo, insert hook in same ch, yo, pull lp through, yo, pull through 2 lps on hook, yo, pull through all 3 lps on hook.

Triple picot: Ch 5, (sl st, ch 5, sl st, ch 4, sl st) in 4th ch from hook.

INSTRUCTIONS
EDGING
Row 1: [Ch 4, dc in 4th ch from hook] number of times needed to fit around outer edges of handkerchief, ending in odd number of ch sps, turn.

Row 2: Ch 1, 5 sc in each ch sp across, turn.

Row 3: Sl st in each of first 3 sts, ch 1, sc in same st as last sl st, *[ch 3, **cl** (see Special Stitches) in 3rd ch from hook] twice, sc in center st of next 5-sc group, rep from * across, turn. Fasten off.

Row 4: Join with sc between cls of first 2-cl group, [ch 3, cl in 3rd ch from hook, **triple picot** (see Special Stitches), ch 3, cl in 3rd ch from hook, sc between cl of next 2-cl group] across. Fasten off.

FINISHING
1. Sew Edging to handkerchief. Spray with starch and press.

2. Turn bowl upside down. Place handkerchief over bowl, wrap crochet cotton tightly around neck of bowl several times and tie to secure handkerchief.

3. Tie ribbon in bow around neck of bowl; trim ends. Turn bowl right side up. ■

Flirty Fans Flower

SKILL LEVEL

EASY

FINISHED SIZES
Edging: ¾ inch wide
Flower: 2½ inches across

MATERIALS
- Size 10 crochet cotton:
    150 yds pink variegated
- Size 10/1.15mm steel crochet hook
- Lady's white handkerchief
- 18 inches florist's wire
- Spray starch

INSTRUCTIONS
EDGING
Place slip knot on hook and insert hook through fabric on outer edge of handkerchief, yo, pull lp through, yo, complete as sc, ch 5, (dc, ch 1) 4 times in 5th ch from hook, spacing sts ½ inch apart, [sc, ch 5, (dc, ch 1) 4 times in 5th ch from hook] around, join with sl st in beg sc. Fasten off.

FINISHING
1. Spray with starch and press.

2. Gather and twist handkerchief tog below Edging to form stem (see photo).

3. Wrap florist's wire around twisted stem to secure. ■

Tiny Tiaras
Flower

SKILL LEVEL

EASY

FINISHED SIZES
Edging: ⅝ inch wide
Flower: 2½ inches across

MATERIALS
- Size 10 crochet cotton:
    150 yds pink
- Size 10/1.15mm steel crochet hook
- Sewing needle
- Lady's pink floral handkerchief
- 18 inches florist's wire
- Pink sewing thread
- Spray starch

SPECIAL STITCH
Shell: (2 dc, ch 2, 2 dc) in designated ch sp.

INSTRUCTIONS
EDGING
Row 1: Ch 4, **shell** *(see Special Stitch)* in 4th ch from hook, turn. *(1 shell)*

Rows 2–4: Ch 3, shell in ch sp of next shell, turn.

Row 5: Ch 3, shell in next shell, working in end of rows, ch 1, (dc, ch 1) 5 times in next ch-3 sp, sc in next ch-3 sp, **turn**, ch 3, sk next ch-1 sp, [sc in next ch-1 sp, ch 3] 4 times, sc in next ch-1 sp, shell in next shell, turn.

Row 6: Ch 3, shell in next shell, leaving rem sts unworked, turn.

Row 7: Ch 2, shell in next shell, turn.

Next rows: Rep rows 5–7 consecutively until piece measures the same as outer edge of handkerchief. Fasten off at end of last row.

FINISHING
1. Sew Edging to outer edge of handkerchief.

2. Spray with starch and press.

3. Gather and twist handkerchief tog below Edging to form stem *(see photo)*.

4. Wrap florist's wire around twisted stem to secure. ■

Romantic Ruffles Flower

SKILL LEVEL

EASY

FINISHED SIZES
Edging: ⅝ inch wide
Flower: 3 inches across

MATERIALS
- Size 10 crochet cotton: 150 yds pink
- Size 10/1.15mm steel crochet hook
- Lady's white handkerchief
- 18 inches florist's wire
- Spray starch

PATTERN NOTE
Join with slip stitch as indicated unless otherwise stated.

INSTRUCTIONS
EDGING
Rnd 1: Place slip knot on hook and insert hook through fabric on outer edge of handkerchief, yo, pull lp through, yo, complete as sc, ch 3, sp st about ⅜ inch apart, (sc, ch 3) around outer edge of handkerchief with (sc, ch 3) twice in each corner, **join** (see Pattern Note) in beg sc.

Rnd 2: Sl st in first ch sp, **ch 4** (counts as first dc and ch-1 sp), (dc, ch 1) twice in same sp, (dc, ch 1) 3 times in each ch sp around, join in 3rd ch of beg ch-4.

Rnd 3: (Sl st, ch 1, sc) in first ch sp, ch 3, (sc, ch 3) in each ch sp around, join in beg sc. Fasten off.

FINISHING
1. Spray with starch and press.
2. Gather and twist handkerchief tog below Edging to form stem (see photo).
3. Wrap florist's wire around twisted stem to secure. ■

Beaded ART NOUVEAU BAG

SKILL LEVEL

INTERMEDIATE

FINISHED SIZES
Edging: 1 inch wide
Bag: 7½ inches deep x 12 inches wide

MATERIALS
- Size 10 crochet cotton: 300 yds purple
- Size 10/1.15mm steel crochet hook
- Sewing needle
- ⅝-inch-wide purple ribbon: 1 yd
- Purple ¼-inch long oval beads: approximately 200
- Lady's lavender handkerchiefs: 2 with same measurements
- Purple sewing thread

SPECIAL STITCHES
Love knot: Pull up a ½-inch lp on hook, yo, pull lp through, sc in back strand of long lp *(see Fig. 1)*.

Double love knot: *Pull up a ½-inch lp on hook, yo, pull lp through, sc in back strand of long lp *(see Fig. 1)*, rep from * *(see Fig. 2)*.

Shell: (3 dc, ch 2, 3 dc) in designated place.

Cluster (cl): Yo, insert hook in designated place, yo, pull lp through, yo, pull through 2 lps on hook, [yo, insert hook in same place, yo, pull lp through, yo, pull through 2 lps on hook] twice, yo, pull through all 4 lps on hook.

Fig. 1
Love Knot

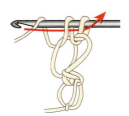
Fig. 2
Double Love Knot

INSTRUCTIONS
EDGING
MAKE 2.
Row 1: [Ch 4, tr in 4th ch from hook] number of times needed to fit around outer edge of handkerchief, turn.

Row 2: (Sl st, ch 1, 5 sc) in first ch sp, 5 sc in each ch sp across, **do not turn**. Fasten off.

Note: Thread 100 beads onto crochet cotton; push back until needed.

Row 3: Join with sl st in center sc of first 5-sc group, [**double love knot** *(see Special Stitches)*, ch 1, pull up 1 bead, ch 1, **love knot** *(see Special Stitches)*, sc in center sc of last double love knot, love knot, sc in center st of next 5-sc group] across. Fasten off.

Sew 1 Edging around each handkerchief ¼ inch from outer edge.

PINEAPPLE APPLIQUÉ
Row 1: Ch 4, (2 dc, {ch 2, 3 dc} twice) in 4th ch from hook *(first 3 chs count as first dc)*, turn. *(9 dc, 2 ch sps)*

Row 2: Ch 3, **shell** *(see Special Stitches)* in first ch sp, ch 2, shell in last ch sp, turn. *(2 shells, 1 ch-2 sp)*

Row 3: Ch 3, shell in ch sp of first shell, ch 2, shell in next ch-2 sp, ch 2, shell in ch sp of last shell, turn. *(3 shells, 2 ch-2 sps)*

Row 4: Ch 3, shell in first shell, ch 4, 12 tr in next shell, ch 4, shell in last shell, turn. *(12 tr, 2 shells, 2 ch-4 sps)*

Row 5: Ch 3, shell in first shell, ch 4, dc in next tr, [ch 1, dc in next tr] 11 times, ch 4, shell in last shell, turn. *(12 dc, 11 ch-1 sps, 2 shells, 2 ch-4 sps)*

Row 6: Ch 3, shell in first shell, ch 4, sk next ch-4 sp, sc in next ch-1 sp, [ch 3, sc in next ch-1 sp] 10 times, ch 4, shell in last shell, turn. *(11 sc, 10 ch-3 sps, 2 shells, 2 ch-4 sps)*

Row 7: Ch 3, shell in first shell, ch 4, sk next ch-4 sp, sc in next ch-3 sp, [ch 3, sc in next ch-3 sp] 9 times, ch 4, shell in last shell, turn. *(10 sc, 9 ch-3 sps, 2 shells, 2 ch-4 sps)*

Row 8: Ch 3, shell in first shell, ch 4, sk next ch-4 sp, sc in next ch-3 sp, [ch 3, sc in next ch-3 sp] 8 times, ch 4, shell in last shell, turn. *(9 sc, 8 ch-3 sps, 2 shells, 2 ch-4 sps)*

Row 9: Ch 3, shell in first shell, ch 4, sk next ch-4 sp, sc in next ch-3 sp, [ch 3, sc in next ch-3 sp] 7 times, ch 4, shell in last shell, turn. *(8 sc, 7 ch-3 sps, 2 shells, 2 ch-4 sps)*

Row 10: Ch 3, shell in first shell, ch 4, sk next ch-4 sp, sc in next ch-3 sp, [ch 3, sc in next ch-3 sp] 6 times, ch 4, shell in last shell, turn. *(7 sc, 6 ch-3 sps, 2 shells, 2 ch-4 sps)*

Row 11: Ch 3, shell in first shell, ch 4, sk next ch-4 sp, sc in next ch-3 sp, [ch 3, sc in next ch-3 sp] 5 times, ch 4, shell in last shell, turn. *(6 sc, 5 ch-3 sps, 2 shells, 2 ch-4 sps)*

Row 12: Ch 3, shell in first shell, ch 4, sk next ch-4 sp, sc in next ch-3 sp, [ch 3, sc in next ch-3 sp] 4 times, ch 4, shell in last shell, turn. *(5 sc, 4 ch-3 sps, 2 shells, 2 ch-4 sps)*

Row 13: Ch 3, shell in first shell, ch 4, sk next ch-4 sp, sc in next ch-3 sp, [ch 3, sc in next ch-3 sp] 3 times, ch 4, shell in last shell, turn. *(4 sc, 3 ch-3 sps, 2 shells, 2 ch-4 sps)*

Row 14: Ch 3, shell in first shell, ch 4, sk next ch-4 sp, sc in next ch-3 sp, [ch 3, sc in next ch-3 sp] twice, ch 4, shell in last shell, turn. *(3 sc, 2 ch-3 sps, 2 shells, 2 ch-4 sps)*

Row 15: Ch 3, shell in first shell, ch 4, sk next ch-4 sp, sc in next ch-3 sp, ch 3, sc in next ch-3 sp, ch 4, shell in last shell, turn. *(2 shells, 2 sc, 2 ch-4 sps, 1 ch-3 sp)*

Row 16: Ch 3, shell in first shell, ch 4, sk next ch-4 sp, sc in next ch-3 sp, ch 4, shell in last shell, turn. *(2 shells, 2 ch-4 sps, 1 sc)*

Row 17: Ch 3, shell in first shell, ch 4, sc in next sc, ch 4, shell in last shell, turn.

Row 18: Ch 3, **cl** *(see Special Stitches)* in each of next 2 shells, ch 3, sl st in last st. Fasten off.

FINISHING

1. Matching 1 corner to opposite corner, fold each handkerchief in half, forming a triangle, press.

2. Sew across each triangle, 1 inch from fold, forming a casing.

3. Holding handkerchiefs tog, sew edges of inside triangles tog leaving outer triangle of each handkerchief unsewn.

4. Pull 18-inch length of ribbon through each casing. Tie ends of ribbons into a bow on each side.

5. Sew Appliqué to center of top triangle on 1 side for front *(see photo).* ■

Copyright © 2008 DRG, 306 East Parr Road, Berne, IN 46711. All rights reserved.
This publication may not be reproduced in part or in whole without written permission from the publisher.

TOLL-FREE ORDER LINE or to request a free catalog (800) LV-ANNIE (800) 582-6643
Customer Service (800) AT-ANNIE (800) 282-6643, **Fax** (800) 882-6643
Visit AnniesAttic.com

We have made every effort to ensure the accuracy and completeness of these instructions.
We cannot, however, be responsible for human error, typographical mistakes or variations in individual work.

ISBN: 978-1-59635-230-8

Stitch Guide

For more complete information, visit **FreePatterns.com**

ABBREVIATIONS

beg	begin/begins/beginning
bpdc	back post double crochet
bpsc	back post single crochet
bptr	back post treble crochet
CC	contrasting color
ch(s)	chain(s)
ch-	refers to chain or space previously made (e.g., ch-1 space)
ch sp(s)	chain space(s)
cl(s)	cluster(s)
cm	centimeter(s)
dc	double crochet (singular/plural)
dc dec	double crochet 2 or more stitches together, as indicated
dec	decrease/decreases/decreasing
dtr	double treble crochet
ext	extended
fpdc	front post double crochet
fpsc	front post single crochet
fptr	front post treble crochet
g	gram(s)
hdc	half double crochet
hdc dec	half double crochet 2 or more stitches together, as indicated
inc	increase/increases/increasing
lp(s)	loop(s)
MC	main color
mm	millimeter(s)
oz	ounce(s)
pc	popcorn(s)
rem	remain/remains/remaining
rep(s)	repeat(s)
rnd(s)	round(s)
RS	right side
sc	single crochet (singular/plural)
sc dec	single crochet 2 or more stitches together, as indicated
sk	skip/skipped/skipping
sl st(s)	slip stitch(es)
sp(s)	space(s)/spaced
st(s)	stitch(es)
tog	together
tr	treble crochet
trtr	triple treble
WS	wrong side
yd(s)	yard(s)
yo	yarn over

Chain—ch: Yo, pull through lp on hook.

Slip stitch—sl st: Insert hook in st, pull through both lps on hook.

Single crochet—sc: Insert hook in st, yo, pull through st, yo, pull through both lps on hook.

Front post stitch—fp:
Back post stitch—bp: When working post st, insert hook from right to left around post st on previous row.

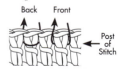

Single crochet decrease (sc dec): (Insert hook, yo, draw lp through) in each of the sts indicated, yo, draw through all lps on hook.

Example of 2-sc dec

Front loop—front lp
Back loop—back lp

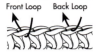

Half double crochet—hdc: Yo, insert hook in st, yo, pull through st, yo, pull through all 3 lps on hook.

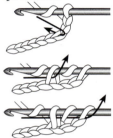

Double crochet—dc: Yo, insert hook in st, yo, pull through st, [yo, pull through 2 lps] twice.

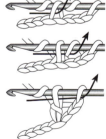

Half double crochet decrease (hdc dec): (Yo, insert hook, yo, draw lp through) in each of the sts indicated, yo, draw through all lps on hook.

Example of 2-hdc dec

Double crochet decrease (dc dec): (Yo, insert hook, yo, draw loop through, draw through 2 lps on hook) in each of the sts indicated, yo, draw through all lps on hook.

Example of 2-dc dec

Change colors: Drop first color; with 2nd color, pull through last 2 lps of st.

Treble crochet—tr: Yo twice, insert hook in st, yo, pull through st, [yo, pull through 2 lps] 3 times.

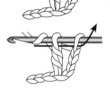

Double treble crochet—dtr: Yo 3 times, insert hook in st, yo, pull through st, [yo, pull through 2 lps] 4 times.

Example of 2-tr dec

Treble crochet decrease (tr dec): Holding back last lp of each st, tr in each of the sts indicated, yo, pull through all lps on hook.

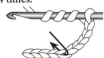

US		UK
sl st (slip stitch)	=	sc (single crochet)
sc (single crochet)	=	dc (double crochet)
hdc (half double crochet)	=	htr (half treble crochet)
dc (double crochet)	=	tr (treble crochet)
tr (treble crochet)	=	dtr (double treble crochet)
dtr (double treble crochet)	=	ttr (triple treble crochet)
skip	=	miss